I(S 10/14

D0120776

THE ONE PAGE BUSINESS STRATEGY

THE ONE PAGE

BUSINESS

STRATEGY

Streamline your business plan in four simple steps

MARC VAN ECK & ELLEN LEENHOUTS

Harlow, England • London • New York • Boston • San Francisco • Toronto • Sydney • Auckland • Singapore • Hong Kong
Tokyo • Seoul • Taipei • New Delhi • Cape Town • São Paulo • Mexico City • Madrid • Amsterdam • Munich • Paris • Milan

PEARSON EDUCATION LIMITED
Edinburgh Gate
Harlow CM20 2JE
United Kingdom
Tel: +44 (0)1279 623623
Web: www.pearson.com/uk

First published 2014 (print and electronic)

© Pearson Benelux 2014 (print and electronic)

Authorised translation from the Dutch language edition,
entitled Businessplan op 1 A4 by Marc van Eck a.o., published
by Pearson Benelux, Copyright © 2012

The rights of Marc van Eck and Ellen Leenhouts to be identified
as authors of this work have been asserted by them in
accordance with the Copyright, Designs and Patents Act 1988.

Pearson Education is not responsible for the content of third-
party internet sites.

ISBN: 978-1-292-00962-9 (print)
       978-1-292-00964-3 (PDF)
       978-1-292-00965-0 (ePub)
       978-1-292-00963-6 (eText)

British Library Cataloguing-in-Publication Data
A catalogue record for the print edition is available from the
British Library

Library of Congress Cataloging-in-Publication Data
A catalog record for the print edition is available from the
Library of Congress

10 9 8 7 6 5 4 3 2 1
18 17 16 15 14

Print edition typeset in 10.5pt/15pt Mundo Sans by 30
Print edition printed and bound in Great Britain by Ashford
Colour Press Ltd, Gosport, Hampshire

NOTE THAT ANY PAGE CROSS-REFERENCES REFER TO THE
PRINT EDITION

Contents

Preface

We have based this book on a methodology called OGSM, which is an acronym that stands for Objective, Goals, Strategies and Measures (or actions). This method pulls your business plan together on a single page so that your strategy is clear, focused, easily actioned and easily shared.

The aim of this book is to help you:

- identify your objectives, goals, strategies and action points
- create a compelling business plan using a proven methodology
- display and share your strategy with colleagues and managers
- cascade your plan effectively to other teams or units within your company.

Endorsements

'Impactful, engaging, practical and highly relevant to the business challenges we face today. That is the strategy approach Business Openers have successfully applied in so many companies throughout the 13 years of their existence, and which they have now captured in this practical book.

I have known Business Openers since their creation in 2001, and OGSM quickly became a key element of their success. Their approach has only improved over time, and it has been demonstrated to work very effectively in setting direction and making the aligned strategic actions happen in reality.

When reflecting on this, I believe there are at least three reasons for this success.

First, in the volatile and changing world in which companies now operate, it is pivotal to define a clear strategy with an aligned business plan. The OGSM approach enforces making clear choices from an abundance of options. Moreover, it guarantees sharp decisions are made that are easy to communicate and thus create the necessary alignment in our empowered and virtual organisations of today.

Second, Business Openers have simplified a strategy-building process that is more commonly considered complex, time consuming and tiring. It takes a touch of genius to make complex matters simple, tangible, and easy to implement.

Finally, co-creation lies at the heart of the OGSM approach. The way Business Openers support companies begins with this team dynamic. As a result, team members own the outcome, creating collaborative energy that results in excellent execution.

I recommend this book highly as a must-read for anyone who wants to make a strategic plan that delivers results, whether for business, for career planning, or for your personal life.

Transforming your dream into a reality has come one step closer.'

Conny Braams
Senior Vice President Operations, Unilever Food Solutions Asia, Africa,
Middle East

'OGSM is a fantastic way for an organisation to define and achieve its goals. After having been exposed to the OGSM approach many years ago at Procter & Gamble, I decided to use it again at Endemol.

Procter & Gamble and Endemol are very different in many respects, but both companies apply OGSM successfully. Why? Because OGSM is a tool that works if you're serious about it.

There are many reasons why OGSM works. In my opinion, three of them are vital. First, it is a practical tool. Individuals grasp it and use it almost instantly; in today's fast-paced world that's a plus. Second, OGSM ignores borders, and works well across cultures. At Endemol, we have rolled it out to all corners of the world: from Sydney to Madrid, and from Mumbai to Los Angeles, people have embraced it and implemented it. Third, OGSM inspires and binds people. It's like a language: content and form go together.

A fourth reason why Endemol has rolled out OGSM so successfully is that we asked Business Openers, *the* experts on OGSM, to assist us. They didn't take over responsibility; they challenged us, and provided a helpful perspective. Our people remained owners of the outcome, and that is critical, but Business Openers coached them to be their best.

What I like about OGSM is that it forces choices and decisions. What is it that we do? And, even more important, what is it that we don't do (anymore)? This is very powerful, as it eliminates waste, and so frees up time and resources to do what really matters.

OGSM is not for the faint-hearted. It leads to discussions – sometimes ferocious ones – and to tough choices. It is worth it, though. I am convinced that it creates value for Endemol at many levels, and across the entire organisation. I am equally convinced that it will create value for other organisations that dare to use it. Good luck!'

Just Spee
CEO, Endemol

'I was first introduced to OGSM during a workshop by Business Openers, and it appealed to me instantly. As a result, I went on to implement the method at Vrumona in 2006.

The logical structure of the method forces you to enter into dialogue with each other in a particular manner, and truly make clear choices. It is much harder to write down a plan on one page and make very specific choices than to write an elaborate book filled with great plans. The beauty is that, once you have finished, the plan will appear very simple and logical, and you will almost forget that you've made many choices and had difficult discussions.

The method's strength is that every word you write down in your OGSM must fit into the overall picture. Unnecessary words or objectives are quickly done away with, which leaves you with what you really wish to achieve, and the way in which you wish to achieve it.

Drawing up an OGSM together with your team is a great team-building exercise, and it can also be easily and clearly explained to all the people in your organisation. It also provides a good monitoring device to check whether you are on the right track, and whether you have designed the appropriate action plans for achieving your goals, so that you can adjust them in time, if necessary.

I still use the OGSM methodology, and am convinced that, if it is properly applied, it can really help individuals, teams and companies to move forward.'

Isabelle Spindler-Jacobs
Retail Director, Heineken Netherlands, and Netherlands Top Woman of the Year 2010

'Impactful leadership results in your achieving your goal. It follows that leadership is about making choices. And, of course, you'd prefer to make the right choices immediately. Unfortunately, only in retrospect do you find out what the right choice would have been. So it would be futile to search until you're sure you've found the right choice. Daring to choose and implementing your choice consistently – that is the key. Whether you are choosing goals for your team, for the entire organisation, for a movement, or for yourself, you have to choose what, how, when and for whom. Making decisions is what strategising and leadership are all about.

The OGSM methodology contributes to your decision-making ability. I don't know of a better method to help you clarify your choices in such a simple and effective manner. The method forces you to be clear to yourself and to each other, so that all you need do is dare to choose.

This book offers you an effective way to make decisions and thus practise impactful leadership. Based on my broad practical experience with OGSM, I am certain that this is the right choice. So, get started now... if you dare!'

Jeroen Pietryga
Former Senior Vice President Marketing & Management Format,
Albert Heijn

'Don't be afraid to fail.
Be afraid not to try.'

Michael Jordan

About the authors

We – Marc van Eck and Ellen Leenhouts – are partners at Business Openers, a strategic marketing consultancy that helps organisations with Positioning (Why?), Strategy (What?) and Internal Branding (How?).

We met at Procter & Gamble, where both of us worked for many years. Because P&G applies the OGSM methodology worldwide, we experienced as employees how OGSM can help businesses and employees to move forward. Over the past 13 years we have been able to help many organisations, institutions, teams and individuals with their business plans, among other things. To this end, we have frequently used the OGSM methodology, and have therefore drawn up a great many OGSMs.

We – and, more importantly, our customers – have seen that the method really works in practice. We have seen how OGSM can change your (working) life for the better. We genuinely enjoy the method, and so do our customers. It's pleasant to work with, not only because you know it's useful, but also because it makes you feel you're gaining control over the things you do. In recent years, with this experience under our belts, we've enriched the method in various ways in order to improve its practicality and substance.

If, once you've read this book, you're left with any questions, please contact us at

marc.vaneck@businessopeners.nl or **ellen.leenhouts@businessopeners.nl**

We promise to reply!

Just one more thing. For the sake of completeness (and also because we are proud of them): The Dutch edition of *The One Page Business Strategy* is a best-selling management book in the Netherlands (holding #2 position in 2013) and we are also co-authors of the (Dutch) books: *The Success of Internal Branding: How to Build and Retain Strong Brands* (2013) and *Internal Branding in Practice: The Brand as a Compass. The Success of Internal Branding* (2008) was rated as a 'must-read' by one of the leading Dutch marketing magazines (*Tijdschrift voor Marketing*) as well as nominated for the Dutch PIM Marketing Literature Prize and *Internal Branding in Practice* has reached its fifth edition, and was proclaimed marketing book of the year by the *Dutch Journal of Marketing* in 2008.

That's enough about us. Let's talk about OGSM.

Marc van Eck and Ellen Leenhouts

Publisher's acknowledgements

We are grateful to the following for permission to reproduce copyright material:

Figure on page 22 adapted from *The 7 Habits of Highly Effective People*, Simon & Schuster (Covey, Stephen, R. 2004)

In some instances we have been unable to trace the owners of copyright material, and we would appreciate any information that would enable us to do so.

Self-test: Do you need a one-page business strategy?

Before you read a book, it would obviously be useful to know whether you'll benefit from it. After all, you have plenty of other things to do, and there are many other books that might provide you with better support. Hence the following test. It is quite simple. For each statement, decide whether you agree or disagree. Give your opinion from your personal perspective, as someone who is part of an organisation, such as the organisation or department you work for, your own company, your association, or your family. Give each 'agree' one point and each 'disagree' no points. You'll find the results after the test.

The statements

1. I work hard, but I don't always feel I'm really making a difference.
2. We have ambition, but in practice not much is happening.
3. There are many ideas, but results are poor.
4. Our organisation's vision doesn't really inspire me.
5. We rarely celebrate our achievements.
6. Everyone always wants more, more, more.
7. We are governed mainly by the issue of the day.
8. We don't dare to make choices, which is why we try to do everything.
9. I could work – and wouldn't mind working – smarter.
10. We have a strategic direction, but not everyone is familiar with it.
11. We have an objective, but it doesn't provide any direction.
12. Everyone tries to reach their own goals, but there seems to be little consistency.

Results

Did you score 0 points?

This book won't be of much help to you. Choose another book for yourself, and offer this one as a gift to someone who could benefit from it. And do please contact us to contribute to the next edition...

Did you score 1 to 9 points?

You and your environment will definitely benefit from this book. So get started; you won't regret it.

Did you score 10 to 12 points?

Forget about this book, and call for professional help immediately.

'The best way to predict your future is to create it.'

Abraham Lincoln

Introduction

Every person has plans, because they make life fun and meaningful. Every organisation has plans, because that is what shareholders, staff and – of course – customers expect. *So far, so good.*

More often than not, though, we fail to realise our plans. This is true both for individuals and for businesses. Why? One of the reasons is that, even in our work, we are often too preoccupied with the issues of the day, and don't get round to executing our plans. Another reason might be that a co-worker draws up a plan without involving anybody, and as a result the plan lacks support. And sometimes it just seems safer and easier to keep on dreaming, and thus keeping your plans vague, or at a distance, rather than take the risk and just do it.

The most common situation, though, is that we *do* have plans, but they're just not good enough. For example, we might have goals that are too vague to give effective direction (e.g. 'To be the best'), or are uninspiring (e.g. 'To increase sales'). So we forget about their providing any structure for our daily activities, or any connection to them. And so, perhaps because subconsciously we know this, we often treat the plans for what they are, and leave them in a drawer. Then we start to despair when it's time for the next year or long-term plan.

During our meetings with managers and marketers, we regularly ask which of the people present think a good business plan is important. The answer is 100 per cent of the attendees, of course. But if we then ask who has a good business plan that leads from vision to action, and is actually deployed as a guideline in the company, a maximum of 20 per cent is left.

In short, there are many plans, but not enough good plans. From now on this will change, because you are in possession of a book that teaches you a method that works. The method is called OGSM, which stands for **Objective**, **Goals**, **Strategies** and **Measures**. It is a method that helps you to solidify your dreams, ideas and plans to such an extent that you will be able to realise them. OGSM is a plan on one page that leads from vision to action. (Yes, you read that right: *one page*.) It connects ambitious goals to concrete activities. It helps you make good plans and execute them smartly, whether at work or in your private life. It is good to have dreams or plans, but it is much more enjoyable to come up with good plans and actually realise them in practice.

Creating a business plan then no longer feels like a chore, and instead becomes a moment to determine effectively, in a structured and strategic manner, where you would like to be in the future, and how you are going to get there. After all:

'Vision without action is merely a dream.
Action without vision just passes the time.
Vision with action can change the world.'

Joel A. Barker

This book is designed to help you make the OGSM methodology your own. And you can do this by understanding it step by step and, of course, by practising it regularly and often. The book is filled with examples, practical tips and exercises. We stick to business scenarios, because practice has shown us that this is where the greatest need exists. But nothing should keep you from using the method in your own life as well: the application is exactly the same. The OGSM method is applicable to everything that you need a plan for. How great is that? So wherever you read 'organisation', we mean 'organisation, department, team or individual'. And where you read 'he', we mean 'he or she'.

You can download the OGSM format as a PowerPoint at **www.onepagebusinessstrategy.com**. You can also join the OGSM LinkedIn group and share your experiences with other OGSM fans.

 To help you create your OGSM you can download the OGSM app. This app takes you through the model step by step; it helps you to put the right things in the right place. You can also use the app to track your progress in time *and* share your OGSM with, for example, your colleagues. Download your OGSM app now on the App Store or on Google Play™ Store!

Now, let's get started.

'People who are constantly looking at the whole picture have the best chance of succeeding in any endeavour.'

John C. Maxwell

Part 1

Laying the foundations

- Since good understanding is the foundation of all great things, the first five chapters of this book provide a brief explanation of what OGSM is, how the method emerged, and how you can get the most out of it. Before you start building your own business plan on one page, good business and brand positioning are crucial, as is an in-depth business analysis. We explain how best to handle this in Chapter 4. To ensure you make clear choices in your business plan, we explain the 'What-by-How' approach in Chapter 5.

Chapter 1
What is OGSM?

Before we go into depth with OGSM, it will be useful to provide a brief explanation of what OGSM is. This will make each chapter, and its connection to the other chapters, clearer.

The acronym OGSM stands for **Objective**, **Goals**, **Strategies** and **Measures**. OGSM is a complete and structured business plan on *one page*. The plan is clear at a glance, and so is the relationship between its various components – the objective, and the ways in which you intend to achieve it. This makes OGSM a powerful tool for monitoring progress and maintaining focus. And its format makes the plan very easy to communicate to employees.

Objective

OGSM starts with a clear and powerful articulation of the organisation's *qualitative* goal – the **Objective** of the organisation. It indicates where you want to be at the end of a specific period. This will often be one year, but it might also span three years, for example. Or it might be the point at which a project is completed. Because the Objective leads everything that follows, it is essential that all stakeholders have reached agreement on it. Thus the Objective is the point on the horizon that you ultimately aim to reach.

Goals

The Objective (the qualitative goal) is then translated into *quantitative* goals (the **Goals**). At the end of the agreed time period these will indicate whether you have actually achieved the Objective. The Goals are thus the coordinates of that point on the horizon – the Objective.

| OBJECTIVE | | | |
| Qualitative objective | | | |

| | | MEASURES | |
GOALS	STRATEGIES	DASHBOARD	ACTION PLAN (WHO, WHEN)
Quantitative translation of elements from the objective	Choices about how to set up resources to reach the objective	Measuring instrument for the strategies	Detailed action plan/ steps

Strategies

Strategies are the specific routes that you choose to reach the Objective. Because the plan must fit onto one page, and because Arial 6 point is the minimum available size of font, you can choose up to a maximum of only five strategies. This leads to focus, and experience shows that focus leads to results.

Measures

The **Measures** consist of a Dashboard and Action Plan. The **Dashboard** can be used to measure whether each strategy is on the right track (and is thus contributing towards achieving the Objective). In the **Action Plan** you translate the strategy into concrete action steps. You agree who is to execute each action step, and when they are to have completed this.

The Objective and Goals set out what you want to achieve. The Strategies and Measures explain how you'll get there. That's how you connect the long-term objective to what you will actually be doing, today and tomorrow.

The power of OGSM is that each qualitative element is followed by a quantitative measurement. The Goals are inextricably linked with the Objective, and the Measures (the Dashboard) are linked with the Strategies. This also makes OGSMs easy to cascade: the OGSM of the organisation can easily be translated into OGSMs for departments or individuals. More on this later **(see Chapter 10)**.

'The achievements of an organisation are the results of the combined effort of each individual.'

Vince Lombardi

Chapter 2

Where did it come from?

OGSM arose from the concept of **Management by Objectives** introduced by Peter Drucker in the mid-twentieth century.

Management by Objectives links employees' goals to the organisation's goals. The starting point is to set goals together, and then feed back results. Jointly agreeing goals that are challenging but achievable motivates and empowers staff. This makes it more likely that your organisation will actually achieve what you want it to, particularly if specific remuneration is offered for achieving the goals, and the general approach is to grow together and aim for professional development, rather than competition.

Drucker developed this idea into concrete steps that translate a clear organisational objective into strategies. These strategies are then allocated to employees, or teams of employees. For each team the strategy is their main objective; they know that if they achieve this objective, they have made an important contribution towards the organisational objective. Each team breaks their strategy down into even smaller concrete actions. In this process it is important to make the best use of the knowledge, expertise and experience that exist in the company, and to be prepared to take responsibility. At each level the goals are measurable, and can be reported on. Subsequently, you can evaluate the achievements together and reward these.

This approach was first implemented by NASA in the USA. During John F. Kennedy's presidency, Americans weren't very proud of their country. Kennedy wanted to change this by putting the first man on the moon. Most of his advisers warned him that this objective was too ambitious; the Russians were far ahead of the USA in their developments in space technology. Kennedy stood firm, though, and then NASA applied Management by Objectives.

The main objective – to put the first man on the moon, and then return the crew safely – was divided into strategies, which were given to teams. So, for example, one team had to construct a spacecraft that could fly there and back, another team had to select and train the crew to reside in space, another team was responsible for the PR, and so on. These teams translated the strategies into concrete actions, which were then given to subteams, and so on. Everyone knew what his team's objective was, and everyone knew that if they had achieved their objective, they had contributed to the achievement of putting the first man on the moon.

Kennedy used to stop by NASA regularly to check on progress, and to inspire everyone. It is said that, one day, he asked a janitor what he was doing. Clearly, the man was cleaning windows, but his proud response to Kennedy was: 'Sir, I'm helping to put a man on the moon.'

After NASA's success, several major car manufacturers in Japan developed Drucker's ideas into the model we now recognise as the OGSM methodology.

It is used by many Fortune 500 organisations worldwide as their main tool for strategic planning. Examples include Procter & Gamble, Coca-Cola and Mars.

We have enriched the OGSM methodology, making it more practical, and adding substance. We have left Drucker's ideas intact, but have added the 'What-by-How' approach **(see Chapter 5)**, and have divided the 'M' of OGSM into two elements: Dashboard and Action Plan. More on this later.

OGSM is thus more than just a methodology; it is a method that has already proven successful for many years. So we were surprised to find that the methodology is still relatively unknown, and, as far as we know, no practical books have been written about it. This book therefore aims to allow more people and more organisations to benefit from OGSM.

'How you climb a mountain could be more important than reaching the top.'

Yvon Chouinard

Chapter 3

What do you need to succeed?

A solid OGSM needs an effective process. In practice, there are two key elements that give OGSM a greater chance of success. It is important to make everyone realise that Support, Content and Technique (SCT) bring success; and that people need to think from their own circle of influence.

The cornerstones of effective planning

'Good things only happen when planned; bad things happen on their own.'

Philip B. Crosby

The success of OGSM is driven by SCT: Support, Content and Technique.

Support

By **Support** we mean that those who will carry out the plan actually stand behind it. If you have a good plan, but nobody feels they have ownership of it, or is inspired to get started with it, then it won't work. This can often happen if an external agency develops the plan without involving the employees, but it can also occur if, for example, the manager develops his own plan without involving his management team.

Content

The 'C' of SCT – **Content** – is fairly obvious. The content of the plan must be really effective, and must fit within the overall picture (of the organisation, for example). A plan that everyone supports, but which lacks substance, won't get you what you want.

Technique

Finally, the 'T': the plan must conform to the OGSM **Technique**. This means that you need to put the right things in the right place, using the right methods.

The rest of this book is about Content and Technique, but here are seven tips for gaining support.

> **Tip** Always create an OGSM together. The OGSM approach calls for a 'helicopter view' and posing critical and pragmatic questions. Experience shows that you can often achieve this better with others than by yourself. And you always need others to implement your plan. Therefore you should find partners with whom you regularly exchange views on your OGSM.

> **Tip** Make a list of employees, and specify:
> * who can contribute to the Content
> * whose Support it is important to have.

Tip On the basis of this overview, determine who ought to be involved in the OGSM process, and invite them to the initial strategy session. Make sure that, during the session, you know why you have invited each attendee, so that you know what contribution to expect from each of those present. If you feel that the people you have invited to Support the OGSM might contribute less to the plan's Content, this is not necessarily a bad thing. It's more important to get their support for the plan, and have them help in its realisation.

The maximum number of participants for a meaningful session is 12. Invite these participants to the meeting well ahead and in an inspiring way. Make it clear that they all need to participate if success is to be achieved.

Tip When constructing a business plan, it helps greatly to have a suitably inspiring environment, with a minimum of interruption. So, if possible, arrange for a location (perhaps an external one) with plenty of light. Give clear guidelines on the use of such things as laptops and mobile phones.

Tip Carefully consider what will work best in terms of date and time. This differs for each organisation and each team, but, in general, Fridays are not conducive to intensive strategic deliberations.

Tip Consider hiring external assistance. There are several reasons why this can be useful.

- If you hire someone from outside the organisation to act as facilitator, nobody else needs to take on this role, and so everyone can participate, and maximise their contribution.

- An outside perspective can be very powerful. An external person can ask sharper questions, and can also be more direct, or even confrontational, in the group process. In this way you can get more out of the meeting, in terms both of content and of process.

- An external person can contribute a lot in terms of content, because he has more distance from the organisation. Moreover, this will typically be someone who has already drawn up business plans for several companies, and can think of cross-connections that might help your company.

Before the session, ask all participants for their commitment. Do this on a one-to-one basis, and repeat your request when the OGSM is finished. In this way you can ensure that nobody makes the mistake of viewing the exercise as obligation-free.

Example

On one occasion we drew up an OGSM with the management team of a large organisation, but cooperation within the team still left something to be desired. In and through the OGSM process they came closer together, and each team member spoke up to support the OGSM. Nothing special so far. But the management team went so far as to formally agree that if they did not reach the determined Goals (and thus the Objective), they would all hand in their resignations, because that would prove that they had not been able to fulfil their management team roles. This moment, which we still vividly recall, is how it should be; for what better way to ensure Support?

(Unfortunately, two months later the head office imposed a completely different course, and declared the OGSM invalid, but that's another story. The moment is no less memorable, though.)

Building on a position of strength

'Change what you cannot accept, and accept what you cannot change.'

Derived from Reinhold Niebuhr

A strategic plan that is created from the organisation's strengths has the best chance of success. So, during the creation of an OGSM, it is important to focus on the things that your organisation can influence, and develop the plan on that basis. Stephen Covey, author of the management bestseller *The Seven Habits of Highly Effective People* (in our opinion one of the best management books of all time), introduced the concept of the **Circle of Influence** and the **Circle of Concern** (see diagram).

The outer circle contains things that we cannot influence, such as the world, our education, our origin, and the past – plus, of course, existing issues or decisions that have already been taken in the organisation, or are to be determined by higher management. According to Covey, we shouldn't concern ourselves with things that we can't influence. People and organisations alike must focus on the inner circle: on what we can influence.

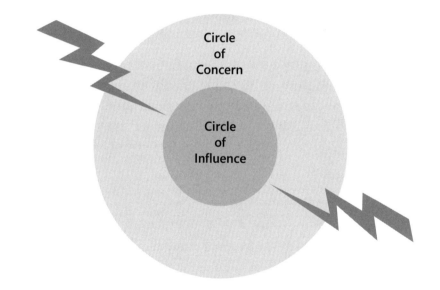

The point is to think from a position of strength, rather than focus on complaints, or behave like a victim. Not 'If we had such and such, then you'd see how successful we could be', but 'Given that we don't have such and such, or that this and that is not up to par, we'll take this action in order to realise our goal anyway.' Many people – and organisations – prefer to transfer responsibility onto external events, or onto others, but it is much more meaningful (and fun) to focus on your own behaviour.

Example (how not to do it)

Conversation at the coffee machine: 'If only I could get better material from marketing, and had a bigger salary and my own parking space, and if only my clients realised that I know what's good for them, and if only I were allowed to give a discount whenever I wanted… then you'd see what a great salesperson I am!'

If we start thinking in terms of the things we can influence, it can be useful to think in terms of opportunities. We often tend to focus on why something is bound to fail, rather than imagine how it might succeed. A meeting is more likely to succeed when it is held in an atmosphere of 'Yes, and...' rather than 'Yes, but...'.

You can help to achieve this 'Yes, and...' atmosphere before the meeting by providing each attendee with an inspirational booklet on thinking outside the box and problem solving, by way of preparation.

*'By failing to prepare,
you are preparing to fail.'*

Benjamin Franklin

Chapter 4

How do you prepare your plan?

A good OGSM needs preparation. Practice shows that good positioning and thorough business analysis beforehand are crucial for success.

Positioning

'A business based on brand is, very simply, a business primed for success.'

David F. D'Alessandro

Before you start constructing a business plan, it is good to know what your organisation's positioning is – in other words, why you exist. An authentic, differentiating and relevant positioning provides direction to what you do as an organisation – to your strategy. Alfred Chandler once said that 'Structure follows strategy'. He had noticed that many organisations were taking their organisational chart as the starting point for creating their strategies, but to him it seemed more logical to first think of your strategy, and then build your organisation around it. Since then, we have come a step further, and now Marc van Eck says: 'Structure follows strategy, but the brand comes first.' Why? Because if you know what you stand for (and with your 'brand' or positioning you provide the answer to this question), your business plan is a logical derivative of this. Your brand or positioning provides answers to three questions:

- Why do you exist?

- What does your customer experience in doing business with you?

- How do you operate?

All three answers provide direction to your plans. For example, if you claim to exist 'To continually provide everyone with access to renewable energy', much like the Dutch energy company Eneco does, then your strategic plan will display matters relating to this. And if you want to do this in a 'committed, outspoken and decisive' way, as Eneco states, this will lead to plans that are different from when you want to do it in a thoughtful, transparent manner. In short, good positioning steers the contents of your plan.

This book is not intended to teach you how to position your company effectively: for this, please see our book *Het succes van Internal Branding: een sterk merk bouwen en onderhouden* (*The Success of Internal Branding: Building and Maintaining a Strong Brand*), Benelux Pearson, 2013 (in Dutch).

Business analysis

'Get your facts first, and then you can distort them as much as you please.'

Mark Twain

The basis of a good business plan is a thorough business analysis that is supported by everyone. A business plan responds to an organisation's strengths and weaknesses, and the opportunities and threats that the organisation encounters. And therefore a business analysis also plays an important role for the content of your plan.

Business analysis also ensures that every participant starts the OGSM process with the same principles in mind. This increases the efficiency of the process, and makes it more enjoyable – which, in turn, increases support.

By starting off the process with a consideration of these strengths, weaknesses, opportunities and threats (SWOT), preferably spread as widely across the organisation as possible, you make the SWOT analysis an essential part of the OGSM process. SWOT consists of an internal and an external analysis.

SWOT: internal analysis

This part of the analysis covers the organisation's internal **Strengths** and **Weaknesses** – those aspects that the organisation can influence, such as employees, image, technology, and product range. It is important that you assess *relative* strengths and weaknesses, as compared with the competition.

SWOT: external analysis

This part of the analysis covers the external **Opportunities** and **Threats**. These factors come from outside the organisation, and the organisation therefore has no, or only limited, influence on them. It is important to monitor these factors and, if necessary, to respond to them.

An opportunity is an event that, if adequately responded to, has the potential to be beneficial for the organisation. A threat is an event that, if not adequately responded to, can have an unfavourable impact on the organisation. Examples of opportunities and threats include market trends, developments in the industry (e.g. the increased use of the Internet), and new legislation.

Opportunities and threats often affect the entire industry, so your competitors may well have identified the same ones. Ultimately, it all comes down to what you do with them.

For each conclusion that you draw in your analysis, try to determine its cause, and whether you are certain (and can thus substantiate) that it is, in fact, true. For example, do you think you have a strong team? Then what makes it so strong, and can you substantiate this?

Before the meeting, survey various colleagues (including who will not be present at the session) and ask them what they consider to be the organisation's two main strengths, weaknesses, opportunities and threats. Put these in a SWOT analysis, discuss them, and then ask all respondents to pick the two they find most important. Rank the answers most mentioned by the respondents in a top five. This will leave you with a shortlist of up to five issues (a maximum of five strengths, five weaknesses, etc.). Take this as the basis for creating the business plan. In this way you will guarantee that the importance of these issues is widely supported, and that everyone feels involved, even if they don't participate in the session.

View the SWOT from an internal perspective, but don't forget to look at it from the customer's perspective, and from your competitors' perspective.

Make sure that everyone names opportunities that actually present themselves in the vicinity, and which the organisation could respond to. The word 'opportunity' is often interpreted as 'things I think we should be doing', and so you will actually be presented with a list of possible strategies. If you miss out on this, it will be at the expense of the 'C' of SCT – the Content.

Exercise

Use the above method to create a SWOT analysis for your organisation. Take plenty of time; by now you must know that this is more than a mere box-ticking exercise. Then put it aside and come back to it later. This will help make your SWOT even better.

The confrontation matrix

With the SWOT you have determined your organisation's position. To make better sense of this, you can develop a **confrontation matrix**. This is a method for looking at how you can use your strengths to realise an opportunity or eliminate a threat, and what weaknesses must be resolved in order for you to be able to seize an opportunity or tackle a threat. In order to do this, make relevant combinations:

- strengths–opportunities
- strengths–threats
- weaknesses–opportunities
- weaknesses–threats

The confrontation matrix provides inspiration for the Objective, and direction to the Strategies.

	Opportunities	Threats
Strengths	Opportunities vs strengths	Threats vs strengths
Weaknesses	Opportunities vs weaknesses	Threats vs weaknesses

Exercise

Create the confrontation matrix for your organisation. For each combination formulate one overall statement. Once you're happy with it, put it aside and come back to it the next day. Tweak where you feel it's necessary.

'Traditional thinking is all about "what is". Future thinking will also need to be about "what can be".'

Edward de Bono

Chapter 5

The DNA of strategic thinking: What-by-How

Making a strategic plan means making choices: choosing the objective you want to reach and what routes you will choose to get to this objective. The clearer your choices are, the more concrete will be the decisions that result from them.

To ensure that everyone makes clear choices in the process of constructing the OGSM, we deploy the **What-by-How** approach. This is a component that we have added to the OGSM methodology, and which helps greatly in achieving truly effective content. For us, this approach goes beyond OGSM: every self-respecting strategic thinker should adhere to it.

According to the What-by-How approach, well-formulated Objectives, Strategies and Actions always consists of two parts: a 'What' element and a 'How' element. To explain this, we'll use a very simple example: 'To get to Rome by hiking'. In this case 'to get to Rome' is the 'What' element and 'by hiking' is the 'How' element.

Many organisations have a 'What' element in their objective, but lack the 'How' element. To stick with the same example: the organisation states that it wishes to be 'in Rome'. There will be a pep talk from the manager that 'We can certainly do this, with all these amazing employees,' which finishes with a 'Let's get to work, people.' Then each team and each person, inspired by their leader's great speech, gets started. One orders airplane tickets to get to Rome; another starts washing his car, because he thinks he might be driving; yet another gets his skates sharpened, because he anticipates a weather change; and so on. These are all great intentions, but there's no consistency.

This is just a simple example, but it is the sort of thing that often happens in organisations. Because the objective offers inadequate direction, the plan itself and the employees' activities are all over the place.

Many more companies have a 'How' element in their objective, but no 'What' element. So, returning to the same example, we have the same pep talk, and the same inspiration, but now the leader tells us only that we will be 'going for a hike'. And again everyone, inspired by their leader's great speech, gets started. One starts to walk to Brussels, because this is a road he knows; another walks home, as 'home is where the heart is'; and the third walks to Santiago de Compostela, because he has always wanted to go there, and it also seemed like a good idea for the organisation. In short, there is no joint final destination, and although along the way you may call out to each other 'Isn't this a great walk?' or 'Together we've already covered a great many miles', you'll never know if and when you have reached your final destination. Moreover, you lose sight of each other along the way.

Finally, there is the combination of 'What' and 'How'. At the level at which the objective is set, it is reasonable to expect to find sufficient knowledge, skill and experience for determining the great 'How'. In doing so, the entire underlying plan is provided with scope and direction.

In short, a solid objective (and this also applies to strategies and actions) is formulated as 'What-by-How'. By describing the 'What' and the 'How', the decision-making has begun. And that is exactly what strategy is all about – daring to choose.

Example

One of the greatest What-by-How objectives ever, as described earlier **(see Chapter 2)**, was formulated by John F. Kennedy, his aim being to make Americans proud of their country once again by putting the first man on the moon.

Kennedy had decided to solve the discontent in America by putting the first man on the moon. So this wasn't the objective, but rather the means to make Americans proud

---

again. You can imagine that only mentioning the goal – 'To make Americans proud of their country once again' – would have been too vague, and if he had only proclaimed 'We are going to put the first man on the moon', the PR campaign would have looked very different. This is an early example of management by objectives.

Example

Imagine that you are head of a department store. Then your 'What' element might be: 'To have all inhabitants of our country regard us as inspiring' or 'To have a large number of fans (or loyal customers)'. But if you neglect to identify how you intend to achieve this, the buyer won't know what to stock up on, and the marketing department won't know what to communicate to the customer, except for 'Become a fan!', and so on. But if you add: 'by offering all the top brands under one roof' or 'by offering hip and affordable design', everyone has a better idea of what is expected from them, and that varies from one 'how' to the next.

Example

Imagine that the national soccer team is playing an important match. Then the 'What' part of the objective could be, for instance:

- to win
- not to lose
- to achieve a convincing victory
- to make the fans happy

and the 'How' part of the objective might be:

- by means of solid football techniques
- by opting for offensive tactics
- by means of counter-attacking football
- by demonstrating individual highlights
- by demonstrating all the tricks they know as one team.

You can imagine that different combinations of 'What' and 'How' would result in very different plans; solid football techniques make for an entirely different game plan than offensive football tactics. But an attacking football strategy and winning massively is also something different from just winning. And counter-attacking football does not necessarily satisfy the fans.

In OGSM we use the What-by-How approach as indicated in the Objective, the Strategies, and the Actions part of the measures. So for every section that concerns qualitative issues. This method is also effective for taking a 'helicopter view' every now and then and assessing whether something is a 'What' or a 'How'. Sometimes you might notice that a 'How' has become a 'What' by itself, or that a 'What' has no 'How' component. But then you'll know exactly what to change!

Now that the process is in order, and the preparation is done, the time has come to draw up the OGSM. We'll go about this as follows. For each letter (O, G, S and M) we'll explain what it is, provide examples, and then provide you with instructions to get started yourself. In the examples we use one 'real' OGSM (from our coffee brand Medellín Secret). In addition, we provide three invented OGSMs, which were designed to be easily accessible for everyone: one for Jeep, one for an A-brand beer, and one for a retail brand.

Medellín Secret

Medellín Secret is an initiative of Diego, a coffee farmer from Colombia, and his brother-in-law Arnold Noorduijn from the Netherlands. It is the first brand of coffee to come from one specific plantation. This plantation is special because of its location high in the mountains, which causes the arabica plants to grow very slowly, producing very hard berries that yield delicious coffee. Diego was astonished to hear how much coffee costs in the Netherlands. He had to sell his wonderful beans at a low price to the local coffee cooperative, and, to add insult to injury, they were then mixed with beans of inferior quality. Together Diego and Arnold decided that things had to change, and they asked Business Openers' Marc van Eck to help them. The three of them decided that the coffee should be shipped directly to the Netherlands, and that they would create a brand for it there. They constructed an OGSM for launching their new brand, Medellín Secret, on the market without any advertising. Without intervention by the global market or by intermediaries, the coffee farmers of the plantation now get both full credit and the money they deserve.

Jeep

We think that Jeep needs a plan to stimulate sales of its four-wheel-drive cars. In the market, the brand name 'Jeep' has become more of an indication of the type of car than of the brand itself (similar to Martini). We have taken this observation as a starting point for the OGSM for Jeep.

An A-brand beer

Our second imaginary OGSM is for an A-brand beer. This is an example that we use regularly in our OGSM sessions. Since this appeals to everyone's imagination in one way or another, it can illustrate the OGSM theory clearly. Unfortunately, we've not yet been able to actually sell this fantastic OGSM to an A-brand beer. But this is undoubtedly because we lack the 'S' from SCT, namely Support; we've constructed the OGSM by ourselves, rather than with the customer. Starting points for this OGSM are that the beer market is showing decreased sales, and that any A-brand beer (after all, there's a good reason why it's an A-brand) is too good to dry up together with the beer market.

A retail brand

As a result of the financial crisis, many retail stores have found themselves in the eye of the storm. Caught between decreasing consumer confidence, increasing competition, late payments and a strong decline in access to finance, many retailers are struggling to keep their heads above water. The choice between a low-cost strategy and product differentiation belongs in the past. Retailers need to be excellent both in minimising costs and in delivering a unique customer experience. Strong brands possess authentic, relevant and distinctive brand promises. Even more importantly, they fulfil these every day in everything they do. We believe this is the biggest opportunity for retailers, as well as for other companies and organisations. For our last example, we have drawn up an OGSM for a retail brand to make the leap from good to great by using the brand as a compass.

'If you don't know where you are going, you will probably end up somewhere else.'

Laurence J. Peter

Part 2

Building your one page business plan

- Congratulations, you have reached the fun part! Now it's time to start building your business plan on a page. From Chapter 6 to Chapter 9, each letter of OGSM is explained and enriched with one real OGSM and three invented OGSMs. Every chapter provides clear instructions to help you create your own business plan.

Chapter 6

O for 'Objective'

The OGSM starts with O for 'Objective'. The Objective is the organisation's qualitative target. It describes what you want to have achieved at the end of the pre-agreed time period. It is that point on the horizon that you wish to move your organisation towards. The choice of the Objective provides direction to the entire plan. Therefore decisions need to be made at this point already. And because an Objective is a qualitative target, it does not contain figures.

A solid Objective meets the following criteria:

- It should be ambitious, but achievable.

- It must be intellectually right and emotionally appealing.

- It must be intuitively comprehensible, and easily restated in your own words.

- Its achievement must lead to complete satisfaction.

  - It must include all essential elements (the 'need to haves').

  - It should not include elements that we do not need to achieve satisfaction (the 'nice to haves').

- It must provide a clear direction (What-by-How).

Ambitious but achievable

Practice teaches that it is better for a plan to be too ambitious than to be too achievable. For if the plan is really ambitious, it will inspire everyone to think more creatively, and this often leads to surprising, inspiring and effective new directions. Objectives that are too achievable often lack inspiration. In this case you can either do exactly the same as or just a little more than you've been doing before; you'll still get there easily, and you don't actually need to develop a plan for that, do you?

Intellectually right and emotionally appealing

'Intellectually right' means that the Objective should be aligned with the higher goals of an organisation, and with the SWOT. For example, it is unlikely that an energy supplier would suddenly start selling lottery tickets. 'Emotionally appealing' is about inspiration. The Objective should be formulated in such a way that the employees really want to contribute to it. (See the example of NASA, mentioned in Chapter 2.)

Intuitively comprehensible, and easily restated in your own words

A good Objective can be repeated by each employee. Moreover, he will also be able to indicate its general message.

Lead to complete satisfaction

Together we must be able to say that, if we reach the Objective, there is nothing left to wish for. This means that the Objective:

- must include all essential elements (the 'need to haves')
- does not include any elements without which we can still achieve satisfaction (the 'nice to haves').

There are no rights or wrongs in agreeing on 'need to haves' and 'nice to haves'; this will be different for each organisation. For example, for some energy suppliers the delivery of sustainable energy is a 'need to have'; for others it might be a 'nice to have'. Satisfied employees are crucial for many service providers (you can picture them saying: 'People are our most important asset!'), whereas for other organisations this is not the case. The same applies to corporate social responsibility, for example. The important thing is that you are clear on what you agree on together.

To determine whether something is a 'need to have' or a 'nice to have', you could use the following question: 'Suppose we do reach the Objective easily, except for this element (e.g. sustainability, or satisfied employees). Would we then truly not be satisfied?' Depending on the answer to this question, this element should then either be added to the Objective or considered as a strategy for later on in the plan.

Direction (What-by-How)

As already indicated **(see Chapter 5)**, it is essential to formulate the Objective as 'What-by-How' in order to provide the organisation with a clear direction.

Decide together the time period for which the OGSM applies. In general, this would be one or three years, or the point at which a project is realised: the shorter the time period, the more concrete the OGSM will be. Some strategies, particularly new ones, can't be expected to be fully operational after just one year, which is when a somewhat longer time period is advisable. But, in general, you'd set the end of a calendar year or the end of a financial year as the deadline.

Objective:	Medellín Secret is a sustainable brand by positioning it as the coffee brand of choice for friends who enjoy life to the full.		
		MEASURES	
GOALS	STRATEGIES	DASHBOARD	ACTION PLAN

Objective:	Jeep is the most successful car in the 4-wheel drive premium segment by bringing back the 'Jeep feeling'.		
		MEASURES	
GOALS	**STRATEGIES**	**DASHBOARD**	**ACTION PLAN**

Objective:	Our beer brand shows profitable growth in a declining beer market by turning the beer brand into a beverage brand.		
		MEASURES	
GOALS	STRATEGIES	DASHBOARD	ACTION PLAN

Objective:	The fastest growing supermarket by fulfilling our 'Customer is King' brand positioning in everything we do.		
		MEASURES	
GOALS	**STRATEGIES**	**DASHBOARD**	**ACTION PLAN**

Example

Here is a quick example of how not to do it, taken from a strategy document of a large multinational:

> 'Our objective is growth in which innovation has a key role when it comes to operations such as production, marketing, communication and packaging. In each of these areas, tailoring to the consumers and their changing needs is at the core of our activities.'

Fine words. They sound like brave management language. But is this also a solid Objective? What does it actually say? The clever thing of this piece of writing is that, on first reading, it seems like an intelligent statement. But if you read it again, you'll find that it's actually quite vague. It is open to multiple interpretations. In other words, anyone can read into it what he wishes to. And that is exactly what happens: everyone simply chooses their own course.

Tip Try comparing the above objective with the criteria for a solid Objective. Which criteria are missing?

Exercise

Think of the Objective for your organisation. First, determine the time period. One year? Or three? Calendar or fiscal year? Have you made clear choices? And does your Objective meet the criteria? You might find it useful to re-read Chapter 5 on 'What-by-How'.

Tip When setting the Objective, it can sometimes be useful to start by looking into the more distant future. First think where you would like to be in, say, 10 years (where do you dream of being?) and then derive the Objective from this.

> '*If you can't measure it, you can't manage it.*'

Peter Drucker

Chapter 7
G for 'Goals'

You make a plan in order to realise it. This is also true for OGSM. Which is why, at the end of the ride, you do want to know whether you have achieved your objective. But as you go, you also want to know whether you are still on track. You also want all stakeholders to have the same definition of the words in the Objective.

Goals are therefore the quantitative translation of the main elements of the Objective. They are the coordinates of that point on the horizon that we have called the Objective. Goals are formulated for both the 'What' and the 'How' part of the Objective: you want to be able to check along the way whether your 'how' is actually bringing you to your 'what'.

As the Goals are the coordinates of your point on the horizon, you must reach all of them in order to arrive at full satisfaction. In contrast to other management methods, in which reaching even 75% of the measurements or key performance indicators often leads to great enthusiasm, it is all or nothing with OGSM. So it is important both to choose clear Goals, and to make them SMART: they must be **Specific**, **Measurable**, **Acceptable**, **Results-oriented** and **Timely**.

Specific

Define what you mean by the elements included in the Objective. In this way everyone knows exactly what is meant by the words used. Describe the goals clearly and concretely, as well as the target group and/or the subject.

Measurable

Now that you know what you want, you must also ensure that it is measurable, so that you can actually 'tick the box' once you've made it. You therefore need to define the goals as a percentage, a measure, or a number, and define with whom and how you will measure this. It is important to have a zero-base measurement to know what your point of departure is. This will indicate directly whether the measurement is feasible and affordable.

Acceptable

By 'acceptable' we mean ambitious, yet achievable. Goals should of course at least be achievable, because if they're not, nobody will want to start chasing after them. But they also have to be ambitious. You need to be prepared to aim together for an improvement that is a substantial but achievable – not 'just that bit better'. After all, you develop an OGSM in order to make a difference.

Results-oriented

The Goals should provide a concrete indication of what should be achieved by the end of the project.

Timely

It is important to specify the exact timing for each Goal. In general, you'll want to have reached all the goals at the end of the time period for which you develop your OGSM; but you might, of course, wish to attain certain Goals prior to this.

Tip	Always include a financial Goal, if only stating that you will remain 'on budget'. There is no organisation that doesn't deal with finances.

You will find that it's not always easy to define the Goals; you should consider carefully the route by which you define them. You can define 'hard' Goals, such as turnover, profit and the like, but you can also set 'soft' Goals, for which you might for instance ask the customer, the team or the Board for an opinion.

		MEASURES	
GOALS	**STRATEGIES**	**DASHBOARD**	**ACTION PLAN**
Sustainable brand: • Average turnover €xx/month • Average amount of coffee sold xx/month • Cash positive • All stakeholders (farmers, coffee roaster, etc.) earn a good salary			
The coffee brand of choice: • 95% of restaurants and retailers selling MS indicate that MS enhances their business • 95% of customers indicate that they are proud to drink MS • 80% of customers indicate that they share the MS story			
Friends who enjoy life to the full: • 95% of customers associate MS with one or more places, brands and/or people that to them radiate 'enjoyment'			

Objective: Medellín Secret is a sustainable brand by positioning it as the coffee brand of choice for friends who enjoy life to the full.

| | | MEASURES | |
GOALS	STRATEGIES	DASHBOARD	ACTION PLAN
Most successful: • Highest market share 4-wheel vehicles > €50k • Number of Jeeps sold > 5,000 • Average margin per Jeep > 20%			
The 'Jeep feeling': • Jeep has the highest brand preference of 'adventurous' cars • 75% of Jeep drivers recommend Jeep			

Objective: Jeep is the most successful car in the 4-wheel drive premium segment by bringing back the 'Jeep feeling'.

Objective:	Our beer brand shows profitable growth in a declining beer market by turning the beer brand into a beverage brand.		
		MEASURES	
GOALS	STRATEGIES	DASHBOARD	ACTION PLAN
Profitable growth: • Annual market share increase of 2% in category General Beverages • Sales of 10 million hectolitres of beverages in the Netherlands, each year 5% growth • Profit > 15% revenue after taxes **From beer to beverage brand:** • At least no. 2 player (market share) in the three most popular categories: ordinary beer, mixed drinks and speciality beers			

		MEASURES	
Objective: The fastest growing supermarket by fulfilling our 'Customer is King' brand positioning in everything we do.			
GOALS	**STRATEGIES**	**DASHBOARD**	**ACTION PLAN**
Fastest growing supermarket: · Revenue > €850m · EBITDA: 27m · Market share > 22% · Highest increase in market share **Fulfilling our 'Customer is King' brand positioning:** · Customer is King: Customer performance index > 59.3 · Brand preference > 80% · 80% of customers recognise brand values · Scores on brand values > 8 in Value Scan (internal survey)			

The Objective and the Goals together form the target you want to meet. In principle, these remain unchanged during the entire OGSM process. After all, this is where you want to go. We now move on to the Strategies. These outline the route to your destination – the Objective.

'Strategy is about choices: you can't be all things for all people.'

Michael Porter

Chapter 8
S for 'Strategies'

Strategies are specific choices about the deployment and distribution of employees, time and money that should lead to achievement of the Objective. They describe how you're going to achieve the Objective (and the Goals).

To return to that point on the horizon: the Strategies are the roads that you choose to follow in order to reach that point. They are your route planner to success.

Here, too, it makes sense to make clear decisions: first, with regard to the number of Strategies. Practice indicates that less is more: you get much more out of handling a few Strategies really well, than from only barely managing a great many Strategies. We therefore recommend that you come up with a maximum of five Strategies, and preferably fewer. And, as already stated **(see Chapter 1)**, the smallest permissible font for the entire OGSM is Arial 6 point. If you need a smaller font to get everything on one page you haven't chosen well enough.

Tip

When you're choosing Strategies, look at the Objective, not the Goals. Why? Because if you take the Goals as the starting point for your Strategies, you'll tend to look at one Goal first to develop a strategy, and then move on to Goal number 2, and so on. This is suboptimal, because a strategy is supposed to work for multiple Goals. And the Goals together form your point on the horizon; it is the combination of coordinates that you're after. If you enter only one coordinate into your satnav, rather than the combination, you'll end up somewhere entirely different. This is why the OGSM model displays no horizontal lines from the Goals to the Strategies.

So put the Goals aside until you've determined all the Strategies. Only then should you check whether you can actually achieve all the Goals with all the Strategies combined.

To ensure that the Strategies are chosen clearly and are well-defined, check each one separately, and all the Strategies together, according to the five Ss:

- specific

- selective

- sustainable

- synchronised

- sufficient

Specific

By specific the strategy should be articulated as 'What-by-How', so that it is absolutely clear what you want to achieve with the strategy (the 'What' component), and how you're going to do it (the 'How' component). It also needs to be expressed in such a simple manner that anyone reading it will know what is meant.

Selective

Being Selective helps you determine whether you have really made a clear decision with regard to the 'How' component. This is the point where you look at what you will not be doing as a result of your strategic choice.

Example

Chapter 5 gave the example 'To get to Rome by hiking'. The hike is 'selective', as we're not going to fly, or drive, or skate. But imagine that we had merely specified 'To get to Rome by travelling'. This is a perfectly fine and correct sentence, but it is clearly not selective. This is where you find out that you should be making sharper choices.

Sustainable

This concerns the Circle of Influence we discussed earlier **(see Chapter 3)**. This is where you determine whether the strategy is based on your own strength, and whether it is Sustainable. Does the strategy truly provide a long-term advantage over the competition, or respond to customer needs, or solve something that really needs solving? A good 'question of conscience' in this regard: 'Would I still choose this strategy if this were my own business?'

Synchronised

This is where you determine whether the Strategies together form a stronger whole than the separate Strategies by themselves. Sometimes you may discover that the Strategies work well independently, but that they counteract each other. In this case, revision might be necessary.

Example

Imagine that the marketing department is building a brand in such a way that consumers will become fans, and are prepared to spend more money on it. But if the sales department then decides to 'dump' some residual stock, so that consumers can get the product for next to nothing from a source where they wouldn't have expected to find it, they can go right ahead and unsubscribe from the fan base, because this won't make any sense to them. In this case, the Strategies in the company have not been Synchronised.

Sufficient

You can use the Sufficiency test to make a critical estimate of whether you will reach the Objective (and thus the Goals) with the Strategies combined, provided they are properly implemented. Of course, you won't be able to calculate this, so you'll have to go with your gut feeling. But since you and your colleagues together know a lot about the organisation and the market, it is safe to assume that this gut feeling will tell you enough. If your feeling tells you that the combined Strategies are not sufficiently robust to achieve the Objective, you should perhaps add another strategy.

> **Tip**
>
> In devising the Strategies, there are five strategic directions that crop up repeatedly in many management methodologies, such as the Balanced Scorecard. This doesn't mean you have to incorporate them in your plan (you may, for example, decide to put innovation on the back burner for the coming year, as you want to put the foundation in place first), but they provide a handy checklist for determining whether you may have forgotten a strategic direction:

- The **market** or **customer strategy** is generally concerned with how you want your customers to think of you, and how you will achieve this.

- The **internal strategy** usually involves Internal Branding: that is, living up to the positioning in the workplace in order for a brand-worthy company culture to emerge.

- The **leadership strategy** indicates what the organisation wants to get from its employees, and how the leaders or managers of the organisation are, jointly, going to realise this.

- The **financial strategy** shows how you are going to ensure that your financial targets are met. This may be a pricing strategy, but it could also include an efficiency strategy, or a strategy that concerns operational information management.

- The **innovation strategy** means every company must continue to innovate in order to stay in the race. This doesn't necessarily mean just innovating in products or services; it may also apply to processes.

Exercise

Come up with four – or a maximum of five – strategies that will help you to achieve your Objective. Use the SWOT analysis and the Confrontation Matrix to determine your Strategies. Make your choices as though it is your own business, you are the managing director and sole shareholder, and all your money is in it. Doing this will often enable a sharper train of thought. Are you already creating the OGSM for your own company? Even better.

Tip

Assign a strategy owner to each strategy. This person will ensure that the strategy is implemented, and thus will take on responsibility for making this specific strategy successful. The strategy owner isn't necessarily the person who implements the strategy completely, because later, in the Action Plan, Actions are assigned to designated persons. Rather, the strategy owner functions as the 'driver' for the Actions; he helps, coaches, compliments, encourages and directs the action owners. And he reports to the (OGSM) team on the progress of the strategy, on any problems encountered, and on possible alternatives or solutions.

Objective:	Medellín Secret is a sustainable brand by positioning it as the coffee brand of choice for friends who enjoy life to the full.		
GOALS	**STRATEGIES**	**MEASURES**	
		DASHBOARD	**ACTION PLAN**
Sustainable brand: · Average turnover €xx/month · Average amount of coffee sold xx/month · Cash positive · All stakeholders (farmers, coffee roaster, etc.) earn a good salary **The coffee brand of choice:** · 95% of restaurants and retailers selling MS indicate that MS enhances their business · 95% of customers indicate that they are proud to drink MS · 80% of customers indicate that they share the MS story **Friends who enjoy life to the full:** · 95% of customers associate MS with one or more places, brands and/or people that to them radiate 'enjoyment'	1. Friends share the story by making them co-owners of the brand		
	2. The Medellín Secret story is easy to tell by inspiring and simple POS material		
	3. Efficient organisation by outsourcing the operation to a major, artisan coffee roaster		
	4. Medellín Secret is accompanied by the right story by sales through the website and high-end independent coffee shops		
	5. More 'friends who enjoy life to the full' are familiar with Medellín Secret by generating free publicity as the cultural coffee brand of choice in the Netherlands		

Objective:	Jeep is the most successful car in the 4-wheel drive premium segment by bringing back the 'Jeep feeling'.		

| | | MEASURES | |
GOALS	STRATEGIES	DASHBOARD	ACTION PLAN
Most successful: • Highest market share 4-wheel vehicles > €50k • Number of Jeeps sold > 5,000 • Average margin per Jeep > 20% **The 'Jeep feeling':** • Jeep has the highest brand preference of 'adventurous' cars • 75% of Jeep drivers recommend Jeep	1. Jeep is considered a differentiating car by a campaign based on the authentic brand		
	2. The Jeep brand comes to life on the shopfloor by aligning the appearance and behaviour of the salespeople with the character of Jeep		
	3. Jeep models are sought after by launching new models with an authentic look and state-of-the-art design		
	4. Jeep drivers and prospects are proud of their Jeep by organising real Jeep safaris and driving experiences		

		MEASURES	
Objective:	Our beer brand shows profitable growth in a declining beer market by turning the beer brand into a beverage brand.		

GOALS	STRATEGIES	DASHBOARD	ACTION PLAN
Profitable growth: • Annual market share increase of 2% in category General Beverages • Sales of 10 million hectolitres of beverages in the Netherlands, each year 5% growth • Profit > 15% revenue after taxes **From beer to beverage brand:** • At least no. 2 player (market share) in the three most popular categories: ordinary beer, mixed drinks and speciality beers	1. Brand preference with consumers by touching them with brand-worthy stories		
	2. Introduction of own-brand mixed drinks and special beers by copying successes in the market that fit the brand		
	3. Great flexibility with minimal investments by purchasing new introductions		
	4. Employees are brand ambassadors by ensuring that all employees translate the values into personal behaviour		
	5. The entire organisation is focused towards the same goal by cascading the OGSM methodology down to an individual level		

Objective:	The fastest growing supermarket by fulfilling our 'Customer is King' brand positioning in everything we do.		
		MEASURES	
GOALS	**STRATEGIES**	**DASHBOARD**	**ACTION PLAN**
Fastest growing supermarket: • Revenue > €850m • EBITDA: 27m • Market share > 22% • Highest increase in market share **Fulfilling our 'Customer is King' brand positioning:** • Customer is King: Customer performance index > 59.3 • Brand preference > 80% • 80% of customers recognise brand values • Scores on brand values > 8 in Value Scan (internal survey)	1. Brand awareness by creating a memorable 'Customer is King' campaign with customers as the board of directors		
	2. Attractive assortment by letting customers select products that we offer with a lowest price guarantee		
	3. Low operational costs with fixed low prices and efficient operation		
	4. Customer feels like a king in the store by empowering employees to give customer support within the boundaries of the brand values		
	5. Accessible stores by combining online orders (clicks) with local pick-up spots in offline stores (bricks)		

'*Measurement is the first step that leads to control and eventually to improvement. If you can't measure something, you can't understand it. If you can't understand it, you can't control it. If you can't control it, you can't improve it.*'

H. James Harrington

Chapter 9

M for 'Measures'

Measures comprise a Dashboard and an Action Plan. The **Dashboard** indicates whether a strategy is on track; the **Action Plan** shows how, by whom and when a strategy is implemented in practice. This division was created because practice showed us that measurements and actions were often used interchangeably within the Measures component. Indeed, the word 'Measure' can be defined both as a measurement and as an action. And because many people seem to enjoy getting just that bit more practical with the OGSM, we decided to implement the Dashboard and the Action Plan.

The Dashboard

'However beautiful the strategy, you should occasionally look at the results.'

Winston Churchill

When we have chosen Strategies, we naturally want to know whether they have actually moved us forward – both along the way, and at the end of the ride. And we don't just want a 'feeling' for this; we want specifically to determine this. This is where the Dashboard comes in. It is the measuring instrument that tells you whether you're on your way to realising the strategy. The Dashboard is thus the quantitative translation of all the major elements of the strategy. Each strategy has its own Dashboard. The principle is the same as for the Goals – that is, quantifying the Objective, only one strategic level down. Again, you make the 'What' component and the 'How' component' measurable. Here, too, it is important to define the measurements clearly and make them truly SMART: Specific, Measurable, Acceptable, Results-oriented and Timely **(see Chapter 7)**.

It is also good to use measurements that are already being performed within the company. Experience shows that it's more effective to use an existing measurement that indicates 80 per cent whether you are on track, than to set up a new measurement that indicates this 100 per cent. Again, ask yourself what you would do if it were your own company? Would you set up a new measurement, or take an existing one that actually tells you quite enough? And if you do decide to deploy a new measurement, then think how you can realise this as practically as possible.

Using the Dashboard will give you an overview (during the execution of your plan) of whether the 'How' component is indeed being carried out. In addition, it shows you whether the 'How' is actually realising your 'What'. If it turns out that this is not the case, you can still make adjustments along the way. After all, as you have already read **(see Chapter 7)**, although you want to keep the Objective and Goals basically unchanged, you can of course change the roads towards them (the Strategies and Actions), if you need to. The Dashboard gives you objective criteria for go/no-go decisions and corrective measures.

Objective:	Medellín Secret is a sustainable brand by positioning it as the coffee brand of choice for friends who enjoy life to the full.		
		MEASURES	
GOALS	**STRATEGIES**	**DASHBOARD**	**ACTION PLAN**
Sustainable brand: · Average turnover €xx/month · Average amount of coffee sold xx/month · Cash positive · All stakeholders (farmers, coffee roaster, etc.) earn a good salary **The coffee brand of choice:** · 95% of restaurants and retailers selling MS indicate that MS enhances their business · 95% of customers indicate that they are proud to drink MS · 80% of customers indicate that they share the MS story **Friends who enjoy life to the full:** · 95% of customers associate MS with one or more places, brands and/or people that to them radiate 'enjoyment'	1. Friends share the story by making them co-owners of the brand	· ≥ 60 ambassadors · ≥ 2 actions per friend · > €400,000 in shares purchased by friends	
	2. The Medellín Secret story is easy to tell by inspiring and simple POS material	· 100% POS material stimulates sharing the story · 100% POS execution	
	3. Efficient organisation by outsourcing the operation to a major, artisan coffee roaster	· Operating costs are no more than xx% of turnover · Medellín Secret has unique position in portfolio of coffee roaster · Distribution network fits the Medellín Secret brand	
	4. Medellín Secret is accompanied by the right story by sales through the website and high-end independent coffee shops	· Sales at independent coffee shops ≥ €xx, via website ≥ €xx · Story is told 80% of the time at high-end coffee shops (mystery shopping) · On website the story is the first thing you see	
	5. More 'friends who enjoy life to the full' are familiar with Medellín Secret by generating free publicity as the cultural coffee brand of choice in the Netherlands	· Aided brand awareness increases 15% each year · > 24 PR moments a year via media that reach friends who enjoy life to the full	

Objective:	Jeep is the most successful car in the 4-wheel drive premium segment by bringing back the 'Jeep feeling'.		
		MEASURES	
GOALS	**STRATEGIES**	**DASHBOARD**	**ACTION PLAN**
Most successful: • Highest market share 4-wheel vehicles > €50k • Number of Jeeps sold > 5,000 • Average margin per Jeep> 20% **The 'Jeep feeling':** • Jeep has the highest brand preference of 'adventurous' cars • 75% of Jeep drivers recommend Jeep	1. Jeep is considered a differentiating car by a campaign based on the authentic brand	• Score on differentiation > 7.5 • Advertising appreciation > 7.5 • > 25,000 visitors on site • > 12,500 unique visitors at dealers	
	2. The Jeep brand comes to life on the shopfloor by aligning the appearance and behaviour of the salespeople with the character of Jeep	• Brand preference customer increases by 12% through dealer visit • 80% of customers experience Jeep brand (values) at the dealership • 80% of salespeople behave in a brand-worthy manner • 100% execution Jeep POS	
	3. Jeep models are sought after by launching new models with an authentic look and state-of-the-art design	• Customer rating Jeep models + 0.5pt. compared with customer rating other cars in the same segment • Expert feedback • > 1,500 new models sold	
	4. Jeep drivers and prospects are proud of their Jeep by organising real Jeep safaris and driving experiences	• 80% of Jeep drivers and 40% of prospects feel 'proud' • 70% of clients and 50% of prospects are familiar with safari /driving experiences • > 1,500 participants safaris • > 10,000 participants driving experiences	

		MEASURES	
Objective: Our beer brand shows profitable growth in a declining beer market by turning the beer brand into a beverage brand.			
GOALS	**STRATEGIES**	**DASHBOARD**	**ACTION PLAN**
Profitable growth: • Annual market share increase of 2% in category General Beverages • Sales of 10 million hectolitres of beverages in the Netherlands, each year 5% growth • Profit > 15% revenue after taxes **From beer to beverage brand:** • At least no. 2 player (market share) in the three most popular categories: ordinary beer, mixed drinks and speciality beers	1. Brand preference with consumers by touching them with brand-worthy stories	• Brand preference 43% • 80% of communication according to consumer in line with brand values • 80% know our stories	
	2. Introduction of own-brand mixed drinks and special beers by copying successes in the market that fit the brand	• 2/3 introductions have larger turnover than originals • Turnover introductions according to plan • 95% of consumers find that the introductions match our brand	
	3. Great flexibility with minimal investments by purchasing new introductions	• Time to market new introduction ≤ 2 months • ROA > 25% • 80% new introductions from external plant	
	4. Employees are brand ambassadors by ensuring that all employees translate the values into personal behaviour	• 80% of clients indicate that employees show brand-worthy behaviour • 40% of employees score 'spot on' on 3 out of 5 brand values (internal measurement) • 80% of employees know the brand values and indicate that they apply them	
	5. The entire organisation is focused towards the same goal by cascading the OGSM methodology down to an individual level	• Employer Engagement score 'strategic alignment' employees ≥ 85% • All departments work according to OGSM • All assessments linked to OGSMs	

		MEASURES	
GOALS	**STRATEGIES**	**DASHBOARD**	**ACTION PLAN**
Fastest growing supermarket: · Revenue > €850m · EBITDA: 27m · Market share > 22% · Highest increase in market share **Fulfilling our 'Customer is King' brand positioning:** · Customer is King: Customer performance index > 59.3 · Brand preference > 80% · 80% of customers recognise brand values · Scores on brand values > 8 in Value Scan (internal survey)	1. Brand awareness by creating a memorable 'Customer is King' campaign with customers as the board of directors	· Spontaneous awareness > 35% · Top of mind awareness > 20% · > 80% connect 'Customer is King' to our supermarket · Media ROI > 33.3%	
	2. Attractive assortment by letting customers select products that we offer with a lowest price guarantee	· Customer satisfaction regard to offer > + 0.5pt. versus competitors · > 45% of SKUs are determined by customer · 100% prices on regular (= non-promotional) lowest price in the market	
	3. Low operational costs with fixed low prices and efficient operation	· > 15% decrease operational costs · > 12% margin · 100% fixed low prices · Stock and procurement system is 100% standardised	
	4. Customer feels like a king in the store by empowering employees to give customer support within the boundaries of the brand values	· Customer feels like a king > 8 (score customer satisfaction survey) · 80% of customers experience the brand when visiting the store · 80% of employees show behaviour in line with values · > 90% of customer support is handled by store employees	
	5. Accessible stores by combining online orders (clicks) with local pick-up spots in offline stores (bricks)	· 60% of population shops in the store in a quarter · > 8.0 on accessibility · 250 local pick-up spots · Revenue > 20% online	

Objective: The fastest growing supermarket by fulfilling our 'Customer is King' brand positioning in everything we do.

Make a Dashboard for each of your Strategies. Define preferably one, but no more than two, Dashboard Measures for the 'What' component, and preferably one, and no more than two, for the 'How' component.

Tip

If you find you can't define Dashboard Measures for the 'What' or the 'How' component, then you've probably not defined the strategy clearly enough. If so, then adjust the strategy. This also applies if your Dashboard Measures are equivalent to several Goals. In this case you're probably repeating the 'What' part of the Objective too much, and need to think a strategic level lower.

The Action Plan

'Good actions are the invisible hinges on the doors of heaven.'

Victor Hugo

The Action Plan translates each strategy into concrete action steps. Just like the Objective and the Strategies, the Actions are formulated in terms of 'What-by-

How'. You also determine who performs each action (one person, with first name and surname), and when the action must be completed (specify a month and a year). This is to ensure that the Actions will be implemented.

Tip

Try to be selective in the number and type of actions that you choose. Consider what actions are really 'need to do' for the strategy to be successful, and remove those that are only 'nice to do'. The danger at this stage is that you might try to cram into the Actions all those activities that are already part of your routine processes. Remember that an OGSM is intended for making choices, and this includes deciding not to do certain things anymore.

Tip

An OGSM focuses on change. So the Actions should not include responsibilities that are already specified in job descriptions (for example, a switchboard operator answering the phone), but only those that will implement change.

Tip

By adding names and deadlines to all actions, you can see how the workload is distributed, and, if necessary, you can modify names or deadlines, or decide to request external help if change isn't possible or desirable.

		MEASURES	
Objective: Medellín Secret is a sustainable brand by positioning it as the coffee brand of choice for friends who enjoy life to the full.			
GOALS	**STRATEGIES**	**DASHBOARD**	**ACTION PLAN**
Sustainable brand: • Average turnover €xx/month • Average amount of coffee sold xx/month • Cash positive • All stakeholders (farmers, coffee roaster, etc.) earn a good salary **The coffee brand of choice:** • 95% of restaurants and retailers selling MS indicate that MS enhances their business • 95% of customers indicate that they are proud to drink MS • 80% of customers indicate that they share the MS story **Friends who enjoy life to the full:** • 95% of customers associate MS with one or more places, brands and/or people that to them radiate 'enjoyment'	1. Friends share the story by making them co-owners of the brand	• ≥ 60 ambassadors • ≥ 2 actions per friend • > €400,000 in shares purchased by friends	• Medellín Secret has friends by making 'friend wish list' and approaching these • Co-ownership is attractive to all parties by preparing financial plan • Ambassadors feel involved by organising informal meetings twice a year • Friend shareholders receive appropriate reward by paying dividend in coffee • Friends help to make the brand successful by organising a marketing council each month with a specific topic
	2. The Medellín Secret story is easy to tell by inspiring and simple POS material	• 100% POS material stimulates sharing the story • 100% POS execution	• Inspiring sales pitch by taking the corporate story as the basis • The product tells the story by developing distinctive and brand-worthy coffee packaging and display • Functional POS material that tells the story by developing Medellín Secret cups, sugar bags and water glasses • Story is also available in writing by creating a small flyer
	3. Efficient organisation by outsourcing the operation to a major, artisan coffee roaster	• Operating costs are no more than xx% of turnover • Medellín Secret has unique position in portfolio of coffee roaster • Distribution network fits the Medellín Secret brand	• Shortlist of potential operational partners by selecting major artisan coffee roasters with a brand orientation • Operational partner chosen by conversations in which brand feeling, approach and personal click are the decision-making criteria • Successful and brand-worthy cooperation by jointly agreeing on Service Level Agreement (SLA) • Adjustments where necessary by periodic inspection, mystery visits to shops and quarterly monitoring of SLA
	4. Medellín Secret is accompanied by the right story by sales through the website and high-end independent coffee shops	• Sales at independent coffee shops ≥ €xx, via website ≥ €xx • Story is told 80% of the time at high-end coffee shops (mystery shopping) • On website the story is the first thing you see	• Proper network of independent coffee shops by naming and approaching specific flagships • Independent coffee shops are inspired and equipped to sell Medellín Secret by offering regular promotions and tastings • Excellent web sales by offering single-item sales, subscriptions and discount promotions for friends
	5. More 'friends who enjoy life to the full' are familiar with Medellín Secret by generating free publicity as the cultural coffee brand of choice in the Netherlands	• Aided brand awareness increases 15% each year • > 24 PR moments a year via media that reach friends who enjoy life to the full	• Relevant PR by defining relevant approach to the Medellín Secret story (CSR, marketing, sales, entrepreneurship, etc.) and using this to write and execute a PR plan • Multiple inputs for PR by asking friends specifically for relevant, personal press contacts • Targeted PR by making use of online networking (e.g. LinkedIn) • 'Rumour around the brand' by gathering PR expressions on website

Objective: Jeep is the most successful car in the 4-wheel drive premium segment by bringing back the 'Jeep feeling'.

GOALS	STRATEGIES	MEASURES	
		DASHBOARD	ACTION PLAN
Most successful: • Highest market share 4-wheel vehicles > €50k • Number of Jeeps sold > 5,000 • Average margin per Jeep > 20% **The 'Jeep feeling':** • Jeep has the highest brand preference of 'adventurous' cars • 75% of Jeep drivers recommend Jeep	1. Jeep is considered a differentiating car by a campaign based on the authentic brand	• Score on differentiation > 7.5 • Advertising appreciation > 7.5 • > 25,000 visitors on site • > 12,500 unique visitors at dealers	• Relevant advertising concept by taking as a starting point the fact that Jeep has become a segment instead of a brand ('It's not truly a Jeep, unless it says Jeep') • Concept broadly positioned by working out in ATL and BTL activities • Concept comes into its own by placement in Jeep environment (lifestyle) • Authenticity is key takeaway for customer by creating and conducting relevant guerrilla actions
	2. The Jeep brand comes to life on the shopfloor by aligning the appearance and behaviour of the salespeople with the character of Jeep	• Brand preference customer increases by 12% through dealer visit • 80% of customers experience Jeep brand (values) at the dealership • 80% salespeople behave in a brand-worthy manner • 100% execution Jeep POS	• Jeep brand is defined in terms of behaviour and appearance by internal and external research • Rollout plan per dealer by need/gap situation scan at dealers • Employees know what brand-worthy Jeep behaviour is by organising workshops • Jeep dealers have brand-worthy showroom by organising dress-up game with Jeep-worthy prizes • Jeep dealers continue to behave in a brand-worthy manner by use of mystery shopper project on Jeep behaviour and appearance
	3. Jeep models are sought after by launching new models with an authentic look and state-of-the-art design	• Customer rating Jeep models + 0.5pt. compared with customer rating other cars in the same segment • Expert feedback • > 1,500 new models sold	• Top 3 best-known activities through which customers / prospects get the unique 'Jeep feeling' by conducting surveys • Knowing what conveniences clients / prospects would like in their cars by conducting a research • Relevant new models available by combining important authentic-look elements for customers / prospects with the state-of-the-art design they value • Dealers enjoy selling new models by rolling out attractive incentive structures for dealers based on the Jeep brand • Differentiation of new models clear by PR stunts with Jeeps in hard-to-access locations
	4. Jeep drivers and prospects are proud of their Jeep by organising real Jeep safaris and driving experiences	• 80% Jeep drivers and 40% prospects feel 'proud' • 70% of clients and 50% of prospects are familiar with safari / driving experiences • > 1,500 participants safaris • > 10,000 participants driving experiences	• Attractive Jeep-worthy safari by organising annual exploration in particular countries • Attractive Jeep-worthy driving experiences that can be done throughout the Netherlands by developing this together with driving certificate agency and having it executed by Jeep employees • Every Jeep driver has been approached for safaris by brand-worthy direct mail with gimmick • Relevant prospects for safari by Jeep contest and personality test • Jeep feeling broadly conveyed by realising TV coverage of Jeep safaris

		MEASURES	

Objective: Our beer brand shows profitable growth in a declining beer market by turning the beer brand into a beverage brand.

GOALS	STRATEGIES	DASHBOARD	ACTION PLAN
Profitable growth: · Annual market share increase of 2% in category General Beverages · Sales of 10 million hectolitres of beverages in the Netherlands, each year 5% growth · Profit > 15% revenue after taxes **From beer to beverage brand:** · At least no. 2 player (market share) in the three most popular categories: ordinary beer, mixed drinks and speciality beers	1. Brand preference with consumers by touching them with brand-worthy stories	· Brand preference 43% · 80% of communication according to consumer in line with brand values · 80% know our stories	· Relevant and authentic brand values by culture scan in combination with market scan · Brand-worthy communication concept by internal brainstorm based on values · Communication concept is workable by having advertising agency develop this into various expressions · Expressions at the right time, in the right place by drafting and implementing media plan
	2. Introduction of own-brand mixed drinks and special beers by copying successes in the market that fit the brand	· 2/3 introductions have larger turnover than originals · Turnover introductions according to plan · 95% of consumers find that the introductions match our brand	· Successes in the market are known by combining market data with visits to popular nightlife venues · List potential brand-fitting activities available by linking market successes with our positioning/values · Selected introductions are brand-worthy by adapting them to the brand · Good introduction for new beverages by drafting, implementing and follow-up launch plan for each introduction · Successful introductions by monitoring volume and brand fit and adjust actions based on this
	3. Great flexibility with minimal investments by purchasing new introductions	· Time to market new introduction ≤ 2 months · ROA > 25% · 80% new introductions from external plant	· Outsourcing possibilities are known by identifying them · Select suitable outsourcing parties by brand-worthy conversations · Our quality is guaranteed by laying down strict quality requirements and processes in Service Level Agreement (SLA) with suppliers · Adjustment where necessary by inspection and monitoring each quarter
	4. Employees are brand ambassadors by ensuring that all employees translate the values into personal behaviour	· 80% of clients indicate that employees show brand-worthy behaviour · 40% of employees score 'spot on' on 3 out of 5 brand values (internal measurement) · 80% of employees know the brand values and indicate that they apply them	· Employees behave in a brand-worthy manner in the workplace by giving workshops for each team · Brand values are known to management and employees by performing internal branding campaign · Brand values are embedded in business strategy and processes by orchestration to this effect by management team · Suppliers work from the perspective of our brand by having contact persons train them to do so
	5. The entire organisation is focused towards the same goal by cascading the OGSM methodology down to an individual level	· Employer Engagement score 'strategic alignment' employees ≥ 85% · All departments work according to OGSM · All assessments linked to OGSMs	· Every employee knows the OGSM methodology by 'technical' OGSM training for the entire organisation · Each department has relevant OGSM by implementing process by which the MT cascades the OGSM · Organisation's OGSM is definitive by incorporating relevant input from underlying OGSMs · OGSM is a steering mechanism in the organisation by including Goals and Dashboard in PDPs of management and employees · Awareness of OGSM remains active by OGSM update sessions each quarter

Objective:	The fastest growing supermarket by fulfilling our 'Customer is King' brand positioning in everything we do.		
		MEASURES	
GOALS	**STRATEGIES**	**DASHBOARD**	**ACTION PLAN**
Fastest growing supermarket: • Revenue > €850m • EBITDA: 27m • Market share > 22% • Highest increase in market share	1. Brand awareness by creating a memorable 'Customer is King' campaign with customers as the board of directors	• Spontaneous awareness > 35% • Top of mind awareness > 20% • > 80% connect 'Customer is King' to our supermarket • Media ROI > 33.3%	• Specify 'Customer is King' by defining our archetypical brand positioning through the Brand House © model • Validate the customer focus concept by conducting customer research • Create a memorable campaign by briefing the agency with the brand as compass • Select effective media by taking goals, target groups and benchmark results as the starting point • Integrate 'Customer is King' campaign in stores by installing a model of a boardroom in every supermarket so the customer can imagine they are CEO
Fulfilling our 'Customer is King' brand positioning: • Customer is King: Customer performance index > 59.3 • Brand preference > 80% • 80% of customers recognise brand values • Scores on brand values > 8 in Value Scan (internal survey)	2. Attractive assortment by letting customers select products that we offer with a lowest price guarantee	• Customer satisfaction regard to offer > + 0.5pt. versus competitors • > 45% of SKUs are determined by customer • 100% prices on regular (= non-promotional) lowest price in the market	• Customers can indicate their products of choice by developing an online platform • Customers actively participate in selecting SKUs by inviting customers in stores and via social media • Realise lowest price guarantee by letting customers themselves report the lowest price and have close control on these reports • Customers are aware of the fixed prices concept by standardised offline and online advertisements
	3. Low operational costs with fixed low prices and efficient operation	• > 15% decrease operational costs • > 12% margin • 100% fixed low prices • Stock and procurement system is 100% standardised	• Increase HQ efficiency by reducing overhead costs by 1/3 in all departments • Reduce most important cost drivers by implementing LEAN approach • Stimulate employees to reduce costs by valuing their initiatives in a typical branded way • Standardise key processes by describing best practices on one page
	4. Customer feels like a king in the store by empowering employees to give customer support within the boundaries of the brand values	• Customer feels like a king > 8 (score customer satisfaction survey) • 80% of customers experience the brand when visiting the store • 80% of employees show behaviour in line with values • > 90% of customer support is handled by store employees	• Employees know how to behave and work in line with the brand values by organising workshops for all departments • Store employees live the brand by setting up a mystery shopper programme for branded behaviour and presentation • Employees develop themselves by bringing assessment criteria in line with the brand values • Employees feel empowered and act upon this by training and personal budgets
	5. Accessible stores by combining online orders (clicks) with local pick-up spots in offline stores (bricks)	• 60% of population shops in the store in a quarter • > 8.0 on accessibility • 250 local pick-up spots • Revenue > 20% online	• Convert current shops into accessible pick-up stores by adjusting current counters and installing self-service systems • Customers easily order and pay for their goods online by co-creating an app with IT partner • Stimulate customers to use pick-up stores by offering a more diversified assortment online than at offline stores • Improve accessibility in largest cities by creating 24/7 pick-up service

Exercise

For each strategy, consider the 'need to do' Actions. Formulate them as 'What-by-How', and indicate who should perform each action, and when it should be completed.

'The path to greatness is along with others.'

Baltasar Gracian

Part 3

Sharing success and reviewing progress

- Now that you know what OGSM is, and you have mastered the methodology, it is important to implement the business plan in your organisation. Chapter 10 explains how to translate OGSM to departments and individuals, and Chapter 11 provides a practical process for integrating the OGSM methodology into your corporate culture.

Chapter 10

Cascading the plan within your organisation

A great advantage of the OGSM methodology is that it can cascade. This is the process by which the organisation-wide OGSM is translated within the organisation to divisions, departments and people. In this way you can be sure that everyone, at every level, is contributing to the organisation's objective.

Cascading can be vertical or horizontal. You can cascade to any desired level, right down to employee level, which is of course the most extreme and therefore the most ideal form of cascading.

Vertical cascading

In vertical cascading a specific strategy is elevated to an Objective for a department or team. The Dashboard Measures are then elevated to Goals for this department or team. The department or team then comes up with the Strategies and Measures for the underlying OGSM. The defined Strategies are then included as Actions in the main OGSM, with responsible persons and deadlines.

Example

In the NASA plan **(see Chapter 2)**, one of the Strategies concerned building a rocket that could go to the moon and return safely. This strategy became the Objective for the construction team, and the Measures were their Goals. The team knew what their job was, and got started. They did not need to bother with any other Strategies. Building a rocket; that was it for them.

Horizontal cascading

In horizontal cascading, throughout the OGSM it is specified what the contribution of each department or team will be. This form of cascading is used if the department or team plays a role in the entire OGSM. The Objective will then be specified for the department or team. Usually, only the 'How' part is adapted; the 'What' part remains unaltered. This also applies to the Goals, Strategies and Measures, in which everything this department or team has no influence on is removed. If necessary, department-specific strategies are then added, but you need to consider carefully whether they are really needed for achievement of the organisation's overall Objective. The great advantage of horizontal cascading is that the contribution of all staff departments to the business becomes clear – something that has not always been made clear before, or wasn't really possible.

Example

You can imagine that at NASA the Finance department, or the Safety division, will have applied horizontal cascading. The implementation of each strategy required money, and safety was also crucial for the whole OGSM.

In practice, the two types of cascading are often mixed. The line departments might cascade vertically, so that one specific department (such as Sales) makes a success of one specific strategy, whereas the staff departments (such as Finance) might cascade horizontally. This results in a sort of OGSM matrix.

By cascading the organisation's OGSM 'top-down', the strategic direction is known throughout the organisation, and everyone is aware of what their personal contribution to this strategic direction is. This is one of the key success factors for an organisation: that employees know the organisation's strategic direction (and support it) and also know their personal role within it (their purpose). And because everyone works with OGSM, you'll receive 'bottom-up' feedback on how the strategies are progressing, in terms of content and timing.

Tip It is often a great help for an organisation to make a 'stop doing' list, based on the OGSM. This ensures that nobody will unconsciously (or sneakily) continue doing what they have always done before.

Tip Sometimes, when cascading, it might appear that certain departments or individuals aren't really contributing to the OGSM. If so, it is important to determine why. You may have forgotten an important part of the OGSM and need to adjust it, because this department or person has an important contribution to make towards one of the strategies. In this case you can adjust at action level. Or you may have forgotten a complete strategy (innovation, for example) that is important for achieving the Objective. If so, you can simply add this strategy. However, it is also possible that drawing up the OGSM has forced you to choose so sharply and clearly that certain jobs or actions are no longer necessary. In this case you shouldn't merely try to cram them back into the OGSM; instead, you should assign different tasks to the employees – or perhaps just accept that although this department or person needs to do their job very well, they have no direct role in the change that you're initiating with the OGSM.

Objective: Jeep is the most successful car in the 4-wheel drive premium segment by bringing back the 'Jeep feeling'.

		MEASURES	
GOALS	STRATEGIES	DASHBOARD	ACTION PLAN
Most successful: · Highest market share 4-wheel vehicles > €50k · Number of Jeeps sold > 5,000 · Average margin per Jeep > 20% **The 'Jeep feeling':** · Jeep has the highest brand preference of 'adventurous' cars · 75% of Jeep drivers recommend Jeep	1. Jeep is considered a differentiating car by a campaign based on the authentic brand	· Score on differentiation > 7.5 · Advertising appreciation > 7.5 · > 25,000 visitors on site · > 12,500 unique visitors at dealers	· Relevant advertising concept by taking as a starting point the fact that Jeep has become a segment instead of a brand ('It's not truly a Jeep, unless it says Jeep') · Concept broadly positioned by working out in ATL and BTL activities · Concept comes into its own by placement in Jeep environment (lifestyle) · Authenticity is key takeaway for customer by creating and conducting relevant
	2. The Jeep ... on the s... the app... of the sa... characte...		by internal and ... ...rs ...ganising workshop... ...ress-up game with... by use of mystery
	3. Jeep mo... by laun... an auth... the-art...		...spects get the uniqu... ...n their cars by... ...thentic-look elemen... ...ney value ...centive structures fo... ...in hard-to-access
	4. Jeep dri... are pro... organisi... driving ...		...on in particular ...e throughout the ...cate agency and ...-worthy direct mail
			· ...relevant prospects for safari by Jeep contest and personality test · Jeep feeling broadly conveyed by realising TV coverage of Jeep safaris

Objective: Jeep is considered a distinctive car by a campaign based on the authentic brand

		MEASURES	
GOALS	STRATEGIES	DASHBOARD	ACTION PLAN
Jeep is considered a distinctive car: · Score on distinctiveness > 7.5 **Campaign based on the authentic brand:** · Advertising appreciation > 7.5 · > 25,000 visitors on site · > 12,500 unique visitors at dealers	1. Relevant advertising concept by taking as a starting point the fact that Jeep has become a segment instead of a brand ('it's not truly a Jeep, unless it says Jeep')		
	2. Concept broadly positioned by working out in ATL and BTL activities		
	3. Concept comes into its own by placement in Jeep environment (lifestyle)		
	4. Authenticity is key takeaway for customer by creating and conducting relevant guerrilla actions		

Effective cascading within the organisation converts the OGSM methodology into a conscious, concerted and broadly supported movement in the direction of the overall Objective.

Exercise

Think how your OGSM might cascade in the organisation in such a way that all strategies are well and clearly integrated in the organisation, so that their effective implementation leads to attainment of the Objective.

'The only place where success comes before work is in the dictionary.'

Vince Lombardi

Chapter 11

Monitoring your plan

The OGSM methodology can only work if it is fully integrated into the corporate culture. Working with and from within the framework of OGSM needs to be as habitual as drinking coffee.

> **Tip**
>
> In the first year of working with OGSM, it may be useful to add its integration into the corporate culture as a strategy in the OGSM. Indeed, the success of OGSM depends entirely on how it is followed up.

Constructing the OGSM is only the start of the process. And in the process of following up, SCT again plays an important role: Support, Content and Technique.

Follow-up Support

'Individually, we are one drop. Together, we are an ocean.'
    Ryunosuke Satoro

To ensure that everyone maintains their enthusiasm for the OGSM methodology, it is vital that employees are constantly aware of its importance. There are several ways in which you can ensure this.

First, it is important to anchor OGSM in the business processes. You can do this by including it in the assessment and reward system.

It is also useful to provide regular internal communication on progress of the OGSM, both in person and in writing.

Some organisations for which we have introduced the OGSM methodology have introduced a specific icon or title for each main strategy. This is then included in all written internal communication, to make it instantly clear to everyone which strategy it concerns. It also shows clearly that the strategies are interconnected with the operations, and in what way.

Finally, it is vital to celebrate successes, in order to maintain Support: one on one, within the department, and throughout the entire organisation. This doesn't just apply to overall successes; small steps forward are worth mentioning too. So do make sure to also celebrate and congratulate individuals and departments that have achieved good results.

Follow-up Content

'There is nothing so useless as doing efficiently that which should not be done at all.'

Peter Drucker

OGSM is much more than just a format for a business plan; it is a methodology. It is important to position this methodology in the organisation as the means for strategic planning, and ensure that any other methods used previously, such as the Balanced Scorecard, and formats (for departmental plans, for example) are incorporated in the OGSM, or are visibly replaced by it. This will ensure clarity in the organisation, which in turn will enhance commitment.

The OGSM is a living document. This means that you'll be able to make adjustments as you go, if necessary. The Objective and Goals together form the target you wish to achieve. Throughout the OGSM process, these will basically remain unchanged; after all, this is your destination. You choose which path you take to get there with the Strategies and Measures. There can be valid reasons for changing this path during the OGSM process. Compare this to the satnav that calculates the route to your final destination. If you encounter roadworks or a traffic jam along the way, the satnav can recalculate, and provide you with an alternative route; but roadworks or a traffic jam don't cause you to suddenly change your final destination.

The only reasons for changing your final destination (and thus the Objective and Goals) are significant, unexpected changes in the environment, such as an economic crisis, or decisions taken higher up in the organisation and over which you have no influence, but which do affect your OGSM, such as the sale of certain business units – major events, in other words.

Unfortunately, what often happens in practice is that a company might be a bit down on its luck, which causes it to quickly change its Objective and Goals. This doesn't contribute to internal credibility, and thus damages the measure of Support. A better approach would be to call everyone in for a meeting in order to figure out, together, how things should be reorganised.

What works for any situation is to regularly review and discuss progress on the OGSM. Each time, check whether the content and timing of the actions are on schedule, and then review the Dashboard and the Goals. Don't forget to always take a look outside the organisation, and view your surroundings. Has a major new competitor suddenly appeared? Has a change of government resulted in changes to relevant law? What consequences do these have for your OGSM?

Here is a practical process for Content follow-up.

- **Once a month**, organise a short meeting to address OGSM progress in general and, in particular, things that are not running smoothly. Do this for each OGSM. The strategy owners prepare an update on their strategy, and highlight only matters that must be discussed; anything that's going well is left out of the conversation. One person from the team is designated as coordinator, and requests input from all participants prior to the meeting in order to distribute the agenda, so that everyone can see in advance whether and where any issues exist.

- **Once a quarter**, organise a more thorough review, lasting about half a day. Each strategy owner looks at the Actions in more detail (a brief status report on each action, and critical questions from the rest of the team on the progress and quality of the actions, and the influence of the actions on strategy achievement). It can then be determined whether the OGSM needs to be adjusted, and, if so, where. The preparation is the same as for the monthly meeting.

- **Once a year**, plan three half-day sessions for developing the OGSM for the following year. At these sessions you incorporate lessons learned in the past year, and sharpen your SWOT. In this way you can bring your OGSM up-to-date and, hopefully, refine it further. The same is done for cascading.

At every review, it might prove useful to apply the traffic light method (green, amber and red) at each level. This works as follows.

Leave actions that are not yet relevant at the time of reviewing, because they are scheduled for a later point in time, in the colour they were already. Allocate a colour to each action in the OGSM that is relevant in terms of timing:

- **green** if the action is running smoothly in terms of content and timing
- **amber** if the action is not running quite as smoothly as it should in terms of content or in relation to timing, and is a cause for concern
- **red** if the action is not running smoothly in terms of both content and timing, and is a cause for major concern.

All strategy owners must ask their action owners for input, notes on amber or red actions, and their plan for finding solutions.

You can also use the traffic light method for the Dashboard. You should already be able to colour the 'How' component on the basis of the colours assigned to the Actions, but to colour the 'What' component you'll need to gather more information.

Do the same for the Goals. Based on the Dashboard, you'll be able to colour the 'How' component; to colour the 'What' component, again, you'll need to gather more information.

Tip

Naturally, most Goals and Dashboards have only their final positions defined. Therefore simply draw a straight line from where you are now right to the finish line, and then decide where you should be at the time of the review. A 'hockey stick' curve (i.e. staying at the same level for a long period of time, suddenly followed by a significant jump) rarely occurs in practice.

If you and your team decide that correction is necessary, you should start with the Actions, and move on to the Strategies only if absolutely necessary. Thus you create the OGSM from top to bottom, and from left to right but you correct it the other way around. In this way you ensure that the OGSM is corrected down to the lowest possible level, which is obviously more effective than correcting directly it at a high level.

> **Tip** Plan all OGSM meetings (which must be mandatory) in advance for the entire year, and put them on the annual agenda. This is to ensure that everyone will be present. And because OGSM is your only strategic planning tool, the reviews should not be optional, for 'optional' leads to lack of commitment, and this generally does not work.

> **Tip** During the OGSM implementation period, new opportunities or good ideas are bound to crop up. Don't jump into these immediately, but ask two questions. First, would they really contribute to reaching a strategy? Second, would they be more effective than the Actions that have already been defined? If the answer to either or both questions is 'no', then let go of the opportunity or idea.

Make one department (Control, for example) responsible for collecting all measurements for the Dashboard and Goals, and have them report these by means of a standard report.

Follow-up Technique

'He who loves practice without theory is like the sailor who boards ship without a rudder and compass and never knows where he may cast.'

Leonardo da Vinci

It remains important to monitor the 'T' of SCT properly – Technique **(see Chapter 3)**. If, over time, the OGSM demonstrates technical inaccuracies, then this can have serious consequences. The cascading can become less clear, and if different definitions of the OGSM (or of parts of it) are circulating, it is likely that employees will no longer understand each other. This then affects both Support and Content.

Therefore keep repeating the principles of OGSM (briefly) at meetings, and make sure that new employees are immediately familiarised with the OGSM methodology – during their induction week, for example.

> *'Experience is the teacher of all things.'*

Julius Caesar

Conclusion

By reading this book and completing the exercises you will have mastered the OGSM methodology. You know how the method works, what goes where, and how to implement the OGSM in your organisation.

However, as with your driving licence, the theory is only the beginning. The more you drive, the more skills you acquire as a driver. The same principle applies to OGSM: the more OGSMs you have drawn up, the easier it gets, and the better they will be.

You are now consciously competent at OGSM. By using it often, you will become unconsciously competent, and the OGSM approach will be ingrained in your DNA.

You will find that this way of thinking and acting will help you in many ways – not only in your professional life, but also in your personal life.

 We hope this brings you just as much fun and success as it has brought us and our customers. And don't forget to download the OGSM template from **www.onepagebusinessstrategy.com** to get the OGSM app, and/or mail or call us when you would like some remote assistance!